Black O' The Green:

Memories

O' The Auld Days

*Frontispiece: Jimmy Black, on the Hay Rake, ready for Rucking*

BLACK O' THE GREEN

❧

# Memories

## O' The Auld Days

❧

*James*
# Black

Edited by Anna Black


First Published in 1997 by David Roe Publications
ISBN 9528880 1 7
Reprinted 1998

Second edition published in 2006 by Accolade Publishing
ISBN 0-9536238-1-5
*accolade101@yahoo.com*


Tel (for re-ordering): 01505 872889 or 01505 873294


A CIP catalogue record for this book is available from the British Library

Printed in Great Britain by
In•house Printing Services, Dundee University

# Contents

# Acknowledgements

H aving been asked by a few of the younger generation to record how things were done in my younger days, I finally decided to tell my story, as so many of the old ways of doing things have gone for ever. I have been asked to go into detail about the auld ways of farming. I am sorry there are not more photos of the very early days, (my very young days). The reason for this is that it would have been a very brave person who would have ventured into a field at Auchenfoyle with a camera when the work was going on. Absolutely nothing must hinder the work.

I jotted down things as they came to my mind and believe me it was as mixed up as a dog's breakfast. Thanks to my daughter Anna for sorting it out and to Accolade Publishing for putting this new edition into print.

The photographs on pages 57, 64 and 90 are reproduced by kind permission of the 'Herald' newspaper.

*Jimmy.*

*The author and editor of this book*

*James Black*

# one    My Heritage

I would like to go back to the time my grand father, as a young man, came from the island of Lismore. He came with all his belongings on his back to look for work in the Kilmacolm - Greenock area. He was an ambitious man, and eventually started up a contractor's business in Greenock. He realised his need of a wife, and sought the hand of Janet Blair of Auchenfoyle. At that time she had another suitor, Jock Scott of Hillside, and on being asked which one she would take, she promptly replied, *"I'll take the strongest one"*. The duel took place on the bridge over the Gryffe at Auchenfoyle, with Donald Black being the victorious one.

He took his bride to Greenock, and later, when on a visit to Auchenfoyle, he found Janet's brother and his wife not very happy with the way things were going. The wife was sittin' greetin', and Donald Black said to her, *"What's wrang wi' ye lassie?"* Says she: *"Och we cannie mak it pay"*. Donald says: *"Whit dae ye say, we dae a swap?"*

That is how the Blacks came to be in Auchenfoyle. Blair's business went from strength to strength and became MacIntyre Ltd, then Westburn Sugar Refineries ...to-day's Tate and Lyle.

*Donald and Janet Black at the time of their diamond wedding c 1900*

# two

# Settling Into Auchenfoyle

Donald and Janet Black (my granny) worked Auchenfoyle. She was a very hard worker, and I know there were times she had to hide the bottle from him. In fact, years later when my mother was extending the garden, the Irish man who was digging, found a very old jar, with some very old whisky in it!

*Auchenfoyle*

I think he never got over his mistake of handing it over! He must have thought it was explosives or something dangerous.

Anyhow, whisky or not, Donald and his hard-working wife were successful in business and in raising a family, and lived to celebrate their diamond wedding. They reared a large family,

*My father and mother in the early 1920's*

*James Black*

many of whom were scattered far and wide.

The youngest son, Jimmy, married a topper of a wife, Margaret Lang. Now it was usual that the youngest son got the farm, and as the oldest ones got married, they looked for farms of their own. When my father eventually took a wife, my uncle Jimmy said to him, *"As we have no family, we'll just build another house joining this one, and we'll buy land round about us"*. So they took in a few small farms, until they had four hundred and forty five acres.

I'll explain the reason I used the word "eventually", regarding my father's marriage. He was unsuccessful in his courtship with Marion Holmes. She married William Orr of Gateside, and he waited for her oldest daughter! In fact, she was twenty-eight years old before they were married!

He had been shown the need of personal salvation, and, as a young man, accepted Christ as his Saviour. It was important to him that his wife shared his faith. Three children of the marriage died in infancy, but they reared five sons and three daughters.

three

# Early Recollections

I was born at Auchenfoyle on the seventh of April nineteen hundred and fifteen. I was the seventh of the family, and born on the seventh day. Bible students refer to seven as being the perfect number, but my school teacher didn't think it applied in my case, but as usual there were faults on both sides.

I think my earliest recollection is of being trailed to and from West Side school, between my sister Jenny and her friend, Mary Duff, another farmer's lassie. We often walked to the school in our bare feet.

When I started school at the age of five, there were two teachers in separate rooms. The primary one was good, the other one was, well, we'll just say, not so good. It was a country school where the children of farmers, shepherds, gamekeepers, ploughmen, byremen and dykers attended. We had two languages. We used our own in the playground and it was very different from what we were taught in the class room. (At the moment I am writing this as

*The Westside Public School in 1924. Jimmy Black is in the middle row, fourth from the right. The headmistress, Miss Mabel Maclaren is on the left, and the primary school teacher, Miss Bessie Lang, is on the right.*

I was taught, but at times I could lapse into my more familiar language.) My favourite poem at school was *"The Whistle"* by Charles Murray. I enjoyed learning it, and also learned how to make the whistle.

---

## The Whistle

*He cut a sappy sucker frae the muckle rodden tree,*
*He trimmed it, an' he wet it, an' he thumped it on his knee,*
*He never heard the teuchat when the harrow broke her eggs,*
*He missed the craggit heron nabbin' puddocks in the seggs,*
*He forgot to hound the collie at the cattle when they strayed,*
*But you should hae seen the whistle that the wee herd made.*

*He whettled on't at morning and he tweedled on't at nicht,*
*He puffed his freckled cheeks till his nose sank oot o sicht,*
*The kye were late for milkin' when he piped them up the closs,*
*The kitlin's got his supper syne an' he was bedded boss;*
*But he cared na doit nor docken what they did, or thocht or said,*
*There was comfort in the whistle that the wee herd made.*

*For lyin' long o' mornin's he had clawed the caup for weeks,*
*But noo he had his bonnet on afore the lave had breeks;*
*He was whistlin' to the porridge that were hottrin on the fire,*
*He was whistling ower the travise to the baillie in the byre;*
*Nae a blackbird nor a mavis that had pipen for their trade*
*Was a marrow for the whistle that the wee herd made.*

---

*He played a march to battle, it cam dirlin' through the mist,*
*Till the halflin squared his shoulders an' made up his mind to 'list;*
*He tried a sprig for wooers though he wistna what it meant,*
*But the kitchen-lass was lauchin' an' he thocht she maybe kent;*
*He got ream an' buttered bannocks for the lovin' lilt he played,*
*Wasna that a cheery whistle that the wee herd made?*

*He blew them rants sae lively, schottishes, reels an' jigs,*
*The foolie flang his muckle legs an' capered ower the rigs,*
*The grey-tailed futtrat bobbit oot to hear his ain strathspey,*
*The bawd cam loupin' through the corn to 'Clean Pease Strai';*
*The feet o' ilka man an' beast gat youkie when he played –*
*Hae ye ever heard o' whistle like the wee herd made?*

*But the snaw it stopped the herdin' an' the winter brocht him dool,*
*When in spite o' hacks an' chilblains he was shod again for school;*
*He couldna sough the catechism nor pipe the rule o' three,*
*He was keepit in an' lickit when the ither loons got free;*
*But he often played the truant - 'twas the only thing he played*
*For the maister burnt the whistle that the wee herd made.*

Charles Murray (1864-1941)

---

I know that the Bible teaches that if you spare the rod, you will spoil the child. However, the senior teacher was very brutal when using the strap on some wee lassies, and I decided to get rid of it. That was one action I never regretted, although my father made me replace it, and tried it out on me first. When the wee school closed, some thought the strap should be sent back to its rightful owner, in whose possession it remains sixty-five years later on.

When my oldest sister Marion (we called her Murn), was in school there were close to seventy on the register, but between workers moving away, and, in some cases, whole families remaining single, numbers dwindled down to about twenty in my day. There were four in my class, but the other three moved on to other schools and left me alone. I had a class to myself for a year. I considered this to be a waste of time.

My older brother, John, was the only one who was allowed to leave to go to the public school in Kilmacolm. However, when he came home and told my father that his teacher didn't believe the Bible, that finished any hope I had of escaping my bondage. I was fourteen by the time I was set free:- free to a new form of hard labour! Jenny says I was nothing but a nuisance and a torment for a while, but it was not long until I had to get into the work in earnest.

Uncle Jimmy was a terrible man when it came to work! He was very good at getting us out of bed without making us angry. He would get our feet out, and say, *"Come on noo, the rest o' ye will shin follow"*. When I was a boy he would take me out to the drains where I handed him wee flat stones, which he used when laying tile drains.

I liked helping him with the sheep too. I've mind of one time when we had twin lambs and the mother didn't want the wee yin, so uncle tied the two legs o' the big yin so that she would stay beside the wee yin. What he hadn't noticed was that there was a wee slope and did the big lamb not roll down the hill into the burn and get drowned. I could take you to the spot to this day. It was the first time I heard the word *"chawed"*. He said *"He wis awfu chawed"*. I couldna' gie ye a word in English to take its place.

I spent a lot of time wi' him. What a man he was for work! He wouldn't tolerate any unnecessary work such as washing floors, when there was urgent work to be done in the fields. He would say, *"Come on everybody who can crawl. Oot tae the field, and get yer jaicket aff. If yer faither and I wirna' here, ye wid a' be in the poor hoose inside six weeks"*.

Father and uncle were far-seeing men. Uncle said, *"The day will come when you cullins* (young fellows) *will be fleein' aboot on wheels"*. There were very few wheels on the road at that time.

*The first milk lorry*

*This is what happened to me for overloading the bridge over the Gryffe which was not built for such loads*

four                    # Hardships

F or the sake of generations to follow, I
   would like to put on record some of the
hardships of those early days. They certainly
earned their living by the sweat of their brow,
as God had told Adam when he was put out of
the Garden of Eden.

Father and uncle were men of vision. They had
water piped from the Gryffe, which was an
over-flow from Loch Thom, high above
Greenock. They installed a big water wheel
,which drove the threshing mill, circular saw,
hoist (which lifted the corn bags, two hundred-
weights each, up to the loft), a corn bruiser, a
cruncher, which chopped hay for horse feeding,
and in later years, a churn and a dynamo. All
these were worked by a shaft which was driven
by, the water wheel.

I have been told that the name Auchenfoyle
means *"the land of mud and stones"*. Some of
the land was black moss. The fields were
drained by laying a tile drain every five yards,
and if it didn't dry up, they went back and put

another one in between. Even with all that draining, sometimes they ploughed with boots on the horses, as this enlarged the size of the feet to keep them from sinking so readily. Many a time they had to be dug out when they sank up to the belly. It was quite a job when they were yoked to a cart loaded with lime or such like.

Hay was cut with scythes and brought out of these wet places with slypes, just like big sledges. When we were quite young we used to get the job of handing up sheaves of corn to the man who was feeding the threshing mill. This job was often done on Saturday mornings so that we could help, and we hated it.

My father's legs bothered him in later life, and he used to ride about the fields on a wee pony. It would stand close into the gates, so that he could open and shut the gates, without getting off.
My father died in November 1929. He said on his death bed that his brother, my uncle Jimmy, would not be long after him. Six weeks later he died of a heart attack. They had worked together all their lives. Uncle Jimmy and Auntie Maggie had no family, so this left the two widows, my brothers and sisters and myself to carry on the farm.

When father and uncle died, the First World War was over. The boats were not being sunk any more, and our wee island was not so dependent on farmers. This country could import whatever it needed and that would help our exports, so we were starting out at a bad time for farming. We had to work hard to stand still, or go under.

## five
# Finding a Spiritual Home

As I said earlier, my father had realised the need for personal salvation, and when he accepted Christ as his Saviour, he spoke to the minister about it. He agreed with him, and father pointed out that it was his duty as a minister to make the gospel plain, as his congregation was looking to him to lead them to heaven. When he failed to do this, father felt he must leave the church, and find a spiritual home.

He looked to the Lord for guidance through prayer. He then saw the need for adult baptism, but wasn't at that time added to any church. He went to Greenock one Sunday, and followed a man carrying a Bible. By so doing he was guided to the brethren hall in Cathcart Street. Later on, we were taken to the church too.

Transport to church was by pony and trap. To get to the Remembrance, we left Auchenfoyle at 9.30 am, and when we reached Greenock we stabled the pony in the stables in Mearns Street, and walked down through the Well Park to the church of God in Cathcart Street for 11 am.

When we got back home, we ate and quickly changed for milking. Milking was done by hand, and meant all hands on deck seven days a week.

A few years before father and uncle died, they acquired their first old car from a butcher in Port Glasgow. I think the barter system was used, and it was exchanged for a few auld kye. It was a Chevrolet, but having a weakness in the back axle, we had to push it home so often, that we called it a *Shoverolet*.

*The good auld days: Murn and Anna Rorason the maid leaving Auchenfoyle for a day out*

*James Black*

# six
# Women From My Youth

Having gone to the country school, we hadn't mixed with many people, and had missed many of the infectious diseases, but somehow or other we got a dose of measles. The older members of the family were quite ill, but fortunately for me I had a very slight dose. We had to get a nurse in to help out.

I cannie mind whether it was a dare or just an excuse, but I got some soot round my lips and chased the nurse. I took a short cut out of the scullery window, caught her in the garden, and proved at an early age, I wisna' just an innocent country yokel. My sister Murn wrote a fine big poem about Jimmy's first kiss. (That's what she thought anyway!)

Mary was another sister I haven't mentioned yet. I can picture her filling the paraffin lamps, cleaning the wicks and the globes every day. There were fully a dozen of them. Then the dynamo was added to the shaft ... electricity at last! We just flicked a switch, and the place lit up. It was unbelievable!

I would like to tell you about two other great women in my young days, my mother and my Auntie Maggie, uncle's wife. When the new house had been built joining on to the original one, somebody had questioned the wisdom of it. The architect's answer was,

*"If the grace o' God disna' stop twa women frae fighting, fields between won't either".*

There is a story of a man who came for miles on a pony and gig to see the women who stayed in the yin hoose and didna' fight. How true that was. I never heard an argument between them.

*Mother in the garden she loved, in her eighties*

Everybody was so busy they hardly had time to quarrel.

These two women saw to it that everybody was well   fed. They were not like the farmer's wife who had a reputation of being stingy with food. A man said to her  one day,

*"Hey wife, dae ye no ken that an empty sack cannie stand upright?"*

*"Aye"* she said, *"and a full yin cannie bend"*.

*Auntie Maggie Black, Uncle Jimmy's wife, at Auchenfoyle*

There was always a big pot of brochin (porridge) hanging on the swee over a big open fire. The men got a big bowl of brochin and milk and ham and eggs. There was nae time for faldarales. If we kids would say we didn't like something, Auntie Maggie would say. *"Eat it up ye saucy wee rascal"*.

There was always plenty of ham! The wee pigs ate up the scraps and the brock totties were boiled for them too. When they were fat, a butcher came up from Greenock and did the necessary. The hams were rolled after being steeped in a barrel o' brine, then they hung on hooks fixed to the joists of the kitchen roof. The ham was always cut at night for the next morning.

Breakfast was at 6 am, and at 9.30 am a slice of bread and jam and a can of tea was carried out to the field. Dinner was about 12 noon. At busy times, such as hay or harvest, it was sometimes devoured in a hurry in the field. Tea was carried out again between 3 and 4 pm. Supper was about 6 pm. Between the families and a maid, ploughmen, byremen, general workers and often (in fact all of my young days) six or seven Irish drainers, there was a total of twenty-three for board and lodgings. So you can see the women had their work cut out for them.

## seven
# An Untimely Injury

In 1938 I lost two-thirds of the middle finger of my left hand. I believe if it had happened a year later, they could have saved it. It was just before penicillin was discovered.

I had been lifting a box, and a rusty nail went into my finger and caused blood poisoning.

I was in Larkfield Hospital in Greenock for seven weeks ... at least I was supposed to be. I was given permission to go about the grounds. I made a point of being missing when the matron did her rounds, so that it wasn't unusual for my room to be empty. I went across the valley to visit a farmer a few times, and had a wee trip home when I could arrange it. I even ventured to a conference in Paisley one day, and got a puncture on the way home. It wasn't really fair on the nurses who said they would have got their books if the matron had found out.

The best way to find a person out is to call when they're not in. This is exactly what the matron did. My wee love bird visited me regularly. I told the nurses she was my sister, which was true, for in my church we are brothers and sisters, but they thought she must be a very special sister.

Well that is what today would be called being economical with the truth. I did not explain to them that good brothers love their sisters. But I so good had grown that I loved other brother's sisters far better than my own.

I was not like this very shy boy who had great difficulty knowing what to say and how to say it to his girl friend. So one night when sitting on the couch, after a long silence, he summoned up enough courage to say *"Nancy, there is a feather on your dress"*. *"Aye, nae wonder"* says she, *"I've been sitting beside a goose all night"*.

He reminds me of the other fellow who had been going out with this girl for quite a long time, and much to her disgust was far too slow. One day his pal asked him how he was progressing at the courting. *"I don't know"* says he, *"but I'll ask her the next time we are out"*. So they were "roaming in the gloaming" one night and he has his arm tightly round her, and says *"Jeannie, how am I progressing?"*. *"Well, George"* says she, *"judging by the position of your arm right now you are holding your own not so slow, eh?"*.

# eight
# Aspects of Farming

I have been told that the name Auchenfoyle means 'the land of mud and stones'. What made Donald Black leave a good fertile wee island like Lismore to come here, I'll never know, especially if he came from the end which is controlled by the Gulf Stream. The nature of Auchenfoyle land was such that it needed a lot of feeding and draining. In Donald Black's time it was rented from Ardgowan Estates. My father and Uncle Jimmy bought it from Sir Michael Shaw Stewart. There was heather growing right up to the stack yard gate. Not only did it need a lot of draining, but it needed a lot of lime. The wet fields were drained with a tile drain every five yards, and if it did not dry up they went back and put another drain in between them. The tiles were carted from Kilmacolm station with horse and cart. The drains were dug with spades and picks with the help of gelignite. There was no going round the rocks as the drains had to be straight with a slight slope down hill. My uncle was very particular when laying the tiles. When I was a very young boy, I handed him wee flat stones. They were to help to seal the joins. In a very wet part of some fields we laid soles (thin template boards from the shipyards). This kept the tiles even. If we had not done that, and a horse's foot sunk and moved even one tile, the drain would be useless.

The lime was carted from Kilmacolm station with horses and carts, and couped near the burn or schuch (ditch). We aye used the best of lime which came from Buxton. It was called shell lime, and the lumps were the size o' yer fist. It had to be slaughened (soaked with water) with water carried from the burn in pails. When it was wet it burst and boiled and dissolved into powder. It was then shovelled into the carts and spread on the fields, again by shovel. All this work was needed, because it was a well known fact that with a wee bit of neglect the land would soon revert to the wild state it was in when Donald Black took it over. The dung from the dairy kye helped to feed the land too.

The cows were all hand milked in those days. The milk was cooled off in bins which held about two gallons. They were placed on cement shelves in a cool milk house. This story is not for the eyes of today's Environmental Health Inspectors. The folk who drank this milk are the folk whose deaths you see in the Glasgow

Herald. Their ages range from seventy to one hundred years.

Auld Georgie Crawford would be out in Crescent Street, Greenock, shouting his head aff if it wasn't there at six o'clock every morning.

When winter was coming near we would put new shoes on the horses. We aye made siccar (sure) that there were plenty cog holes in the new shoes, about three in each shoe. This precaution was for frosty mornings. Most dairy farmers kept a light legged horse for the milk cart. It was heavier than a pony, but not as heavy as a Clydesdale. There would be about a dozen of these carts on the road. Some of the milk was delivered in wooden butts.

## The Feeing Market

These were the days when men and girls were fee'd (hired) on a half yearly agreement. The farmers would go to Graham Square in Glasgow where the lads and lassies who were looking for work would be lined up. Many of them were miner's weans. The farmer would walk up and down looking for a hardy looking, likely man.

When he saw one he considered suitable, he would approach him and ask him if he would like to fee on with him for six months. If the

---

man had heard that the chuck (food) was not good at his farm, there was nothing doing, and believe me, word soon spread round. This did not apply at Auchenfoyle, as you'll find out later. There were two terms in the year - 28th May and 28th November. If the farmer was pleased with the man or maid, he would ask him or her if he was bidin' on, or ready for a shift. As boys we were aye interested when a new man was coming. If a farmer had a few young sons, he didn't fee the best looking lassie, for obvious reasons.

## Pigs

I was invited to a farm sale in Islay by a farmer friend. I had no intention of buying, but came home with three nice gilts (female pigs). This was the start of pigs at Auchenfoyle, and lasted for many years.

No, I did not bring them back on the plane!

## The Crops

Being a dairy farm we grew some crops. The rotation was that we ploughed a grass (or lea) field. The first crop was corn (or oats) followed by totties plus some turnips, followed by corn, then hay. The grass seed was sown sometimes after the corn was brairded. The seed merchant was informed how many years we intended cutting the hay and how many it would be kept in grass. We got round the arable land every ten

Above: *The three Islay pigs*

Below: *A pig with litter*

years or more. When I write about arable land, I can imagine some of the farmers who <u>have</u> <u>arable</u> land, having a wee laugh at us in this district, picking the wee good bits amongst the rocks.

I'll never forget the time I was on my way to Paisley, passing through Linwood, and those monstrous land movers were scooping up the best of top soil. It was soil capable of growing any crop, with not a stone in sight. What a scandal! What for? It was to build a car factory, and soon the good land became a concrete jungle. When we were ploughing (with horses of course) we were hitting stones all the time.

The man who was termed the first man had to be able for every job. A good ploughman had to be able to set his plough, and make a good furrow. One furrow must be set up against the other, and this made the seed bed. He prided himself in a straight furrow. He had to be able for every job - stacking hay and corn, and work the machinery all for £1.00 a week.

If he was married he had a house rent free, with milk, totties and coal supplied. He had to take the lead, and be first out of the stable in the morning, after having fed and groomed his pair of horses. He could have two or three men following him depending on the size of the farm. The byre man had to be a milker and feed

and tend the cattle. We had a shepherd too. My father saw to it that we did every job. He knew that if we were going to take over some day, we had to learn to cope with the snags we would meet or we would not make good bosses.

We tried to have the ploughing done early in the spring. The frost broke up the ground a bit and made it a wee bit easier to work. The seed was sown by hand, using a sowing sheet strapped round the neck and waist. The seed bags were placed in such a position that the boy who carried the pail had not too far to walk. His job was to keep filling up the sheet with seed. After that followed a man with a pair of horses yoked in the harrows, and that could be a sore job. The seed which fell in the ridges between the furs had to be well covered or it would be away with the crows.

## Modern Ways

Having learned to plough with the horse plough, we had to learn all over again with the tractor plough, which meant looking back instead of forward. The first one we had was a double furrow trailing one. It was pulled by our first tractor which was a Fordson. It was started by a starting handle, and it was fired on petrol, then switched to run on paraffin. Then came the Ferguson tractor with the hydraulic lift and plough to suit. This in my opinion was the knock-out blow for the horses.

Tractors came in in the 30's. As they started making tractors bigger and more powerful, they increased the size of the plough. Being reversible ploughs they start at one side of the field and keep throwing all the furs the same way. That does away with feerins and hints (see the section *'Preparing for the same all over again'* on page 60). The ploughman no longer makes the seed bed. The fur is thrown well over on its back, then a fairly wide set o' disc harrows follows. The seed is drilled in by a seeder with a manure box attached with shoots which take it safely underground, well out of the reach o' the birds.

Apart from pulling up the thistles by the roots, we will just leave the crop to grow. I think I should tell you about a neighbour who had a bother getting a young man to go out and work one wet day. "Look" says he, "there's Jimmy Black oot there pulling jags (thistles)". The roots came out easier when the ground was soaking wet. "Well" says the boy, "if Jimmy Black is daft enough to do that, that is his lookout. I am not daft and I'm not going."

## The Hay Crop

My folk liked to let the second stour blow off the seed before they cut it. Sometimes they grew a few acres of "Timothy" hay. Timothy grew a strong stock which was a wee bit coarse, but easier to dry. It was suitable for horses. Dairy kye (cows) were better getting a leafier, softer kind of hay, and that took more time and patience to get it right dry. This was very important so that it did not heat up when stacked.

The hay was cut by scythe, then turned over by handrakes. By the time I was on the working scene, a solid iron mover drawn by two horses did the job. The cut hay lay in swaths, and when it was dry on top it was turned over by a very clever machine drawn by one horse. It was then shaken out by forks. Before the land was so well drained, slypes were used to draw it out of the wet places on to the higher drier ground. If the weather was not dry enough to ruck the hay, we would quile (coil) it. This was done by making a wee mound of hay. This kept it dry and kept its colour. It stayed there until the weather was safe to shake it out again, ready for rucking. There were times we got caught with an unexpected shower and I can tell you that the one who gave the order to shake out the quiles, was not popular. It was bad enough getting caught with swaths shaken out, but with the quiles, it was a disaster. The loose hay was caud into rows with forks when it was dry enough. We set up tripods (three posts five feet high. The hay was drawn near the tripods with a collector (known as Tumbling Tam) drawn by a horse.

Shafts on the collector lifted, and the whole load tumbled upside down hence the name Tumbling Tam. The idea of the tripod was to keep the hay from being too solid so that the wind could blow right through it. This meant we could ruck fresher, greener hay and save protein too.

I think my folk were the first in the district to use this method with Auchenfoyle land being low lying and damp, we had more need to take all the precautions. Heated hay was a disgrace.

Believe it or not, someone was writing recently in the 'Scottish Farmer' offering some stupid advice to farmers and workers. He suggested that they work with a long fork in case they got farmer's lung disease from the stoor from heated hay. He should have been telling them to get a handy fork and get at the quiling and rucking and avoid all the stoor.

These rucks sat two or three weeks, then they were lifted by a bogie drawn by a horse. Two wire ropes with clasps were placed round the bottom of the ruck and a handle was fixed into the gears at the side of the ruck lifter. A man turned the handle and up slid the ruck.

*This is the way to make good hay*

*Hay ricks:*
*the finished job*

After standing for about three weeks they were carted home to the stack-yard beside the steading. About thirty of these rucks were built into one big stack. We used a horse fork fitted on to a pole about thirty feet high. This was us getting modern because in my father's young days they were hand forked on to platforms, and passed from one platform to another. Right enough, they didn't make them so high. That might have been better for me, because I got knocked off the top of one of these high ones. You can see the height from the photograph opposite.

Now some of you cheeky folk reading this might be tempted to say or think *"aye, is that what is wrong with him."*

These stacks were all raked down, pooked, thatched and roped. They sat there until they were needed for fother in the winter. The hay was forked into hay barrows, (see picture on the

*Haystacks*

inside page) and taken to the kye in the byre. Horses and sheep got their share. Some of the Timothy hay was carted to the town to feed contractors' horses.

## Advanced Ways of Working with Hay

The horses were saved many a sweating when the tractor took over. It pulled the mower, aye, the same auld mower until a bigger hydraulic one was invented.

Then came the machine to scatter it out which meant nae mair shaking it wi' the hand fork.

Sweeps replaced the tumblin' tam, and even a rucking machine was invented and used in the Stirling district. Next came the stationary baler, and then the pick-up baler.

Then they brought out a machine which could pick up eight bales at a time, and lift them on to a lorry. Nae mair nice rows o' rucks, and not nearly so much hay made. Silage has taken over quite a bit.

While all this work was going on. the corn was ripening and many a time it was a case of finishing thatching the hay stacks, and straight out to the corn fields.

### Corn Crop

*The auld tractor-driven baler, condemned by some because you had to fork the hay into it*

In my father's day the corn was cut by scythe. By the time I was working we used the same cutting machine as for the hay, but changed the position of the pole. Two horses pulled it. One

*James Black*

man drove the horses, and another man sat with the tilting rake, determining the size of the sheaves or bunches. The bunchers had about eight or ten bunches to tie using a handful of straw, and they had to be well tied for they had to stand a lot of handling. Six of these sheaves were built together, making a stook. The stook had to be well built, or it would fall as soon as you turned your back. It had to be able to stand a strong wind blowing.

They sat there for a week or ten days if the weather was good. If the weather was bad or there was a lack o' drooth, every single sheaf

*A more modern pick-up baler, with bale sledge attached, but still condemned because you had to build the bales by hand*

had to be made to stand on three legs with an opening to the wind. This was called giting.

One very bad year we put fences across the corn fields and hung the sheaves on them. It was essential to get them dry through and through, or they would heat when stacked. When they were dry they were forked onto a corn wagon and driven home to the stackyard, forked off

*Jimmy Black*
*sharpening a scythe*

*James Black*

and placed on the stack. Now this was a job for a professional.

The heart o' the stack had to be kept high with the outside sheaves sloping out just in the right position. They were then thatched and roped and sat there until needed for winter feeding.

As I said earlier, we had our own thrashing mill, but many farmers didn't. The thrashing contractor went round the country with their outfit pulled by a steam engine. It was quite a day when the mill came. About a dozen neighbours gathered to help out. It was a big day for the women as all these men had to be fed. The farmer supplied the coal to take the yoke to the next farm.

The straw bunches were built into a big stack. The corn was bagged into one hundredweight bags and carried up a steep stair. In my father's day two hundred weight bags were common. That was what separated the men from the boys.

Most districts had a meal mill nearby where they took their corn to be ground into meal. Good old oatmeal for making brochin (porridge) and oatcakes. These mills were built beside a waterfall. The water was diverted on to the buckets on the wheel which drove the machinery. Some of these old wheels can still be seen today.

*Home and dry:*
*corn stacks*

The corn was used for feeding cattle and sheep, but needed to be crushed. The cows could not digest it unless the husk was broken.

### Advancement from the Scythe to the Reaper

The corn is now drilled in and not broadcast. Here I think I should tell you just how auld fashioned my father and uncle were. An old binder lay in a shed at Auchenfoyle for years until my older brothers were curious to see it working. They set to and proved again that patience and perseverance will overcome the greatest difficulties.

---

*James Black*

If ever we could do wi' three hands it was when we got on the seat o' a binder which was pulled by three horses. (The field had been opened by cutting a swath with a scythe all the way round the field, to save it being trampled by the horses' feet). We had to drive the horses and work levers galore. The levers had to be adjusted according to the length of the crop. The flights then brought the crops onto the platform canvass which took it across to the two upright canvasses, then onto the buncher where it was tied up with twine.

*The binder*

The cutting blade had to be adjusted to suit the length of the crop, as this determined the length of stubble. The auld folk didn't leave too much straw on the ground. This is the way it was done for years, then along came the combine. At first it was pulled by a tractor, then later it was self powered. The combine cut a swath of 5 or 6 feet, and was a great advancement as it did the thrashing and bagged the grain.

The next step was a wider cut, and a built-in hopper from which the grain was transferred into a trailer which ran alongside the combine while it was cutting. The hopper was used while the trailer was away unloading into another hopper. From there it was blown into what was called a moist grain silo. The silo was air sealed and grain of about 22 - 25% moisture was kept in perfect condition. As the years have gone by, combines have grown bigger and so has the price. In America where everything is BIG, I am led to believe they can cut a swath thirty feet wide and cost up to £ 170,000. Twenty feet wide is about the biggest in this country. The grain was then blown from the silo into the bruiser, and never handled at all.

## The Totties

The corn stubble was ploughed in, and the field prepared for the totties. The corn roots had broken up the soil, and with the help of the frost, the ground had been made easier to work. The drills were made by a double reested plough, drawn by two horses. There was no wheel on this plough and we had to judge the depth (which was important) by leaning on the stilts (shafts).

If the dung had not been spread on the field before ploughing (and this was not the done thing in my day), then when the drills were opened we brought in cart loads of dung. The horse walked on the bottom o' the drill and we put out a good graipful every few yards, doing two drills at a time. These heaps were then spread with a fork before the planters came along - aye, human planters with strong backs.

*My brother John, using a horse - drawn drill plough*

If the totties had nae sproots we used a brattie (apron) tied round the waist, and loaded up. The totties were placed by hand into the dung.

They were often boxed and we had to be extra careful not to break the sproots thus defeating whole purpose of boxing them. We built the boxes in the byre where the heat fairly brought on - If it was a late spring or too wet and we could not get on to the land it meant they had a start. Then we followed up with a wee pickle of artificial manure. Unlike this modern way of working, we were quite content with eight or nine tons to the acre. Now they expect more than double that, but it's nae wonder this generation don't even ken what totties used to taste like. Now this was a crop that kept us working at them on and aff all summer, keeping down the weeds, grubbing and harrowing down drills and setting them up again even after shaws were up through the ground.

We had to keep renewing the drills and make sure they were well happed up because if the totties were not well covered with soil, the sun would turn them green. (Some varieties were worse than others for coming to the top. They were then sprayed to prevent blight. We placed barrels at each end of the field, and carted water to fill them. We then added blue-stone to the water, and put a sprayer on our backs. It had a tube with a nozzle which we held in one hand, while we pumped with the other. We sprayed the shaws over and under, and hoped it would stay dry long enough to let it dry in. Blight could ruin a whole crop.

We progressed to what we thought was quite a modern way of working. Two seats were fixed onto the ridger pulled by a tractor. A wheel rolled on the ground, and it had a bell fixed to it. Every time the bell rang, the operator dropped a tottie down the chute and the ridger covered it at the same time. When ready for harvesting we moved on from digging them out with a graip.

*My brother Willie and sisters Jennie and Mary planting totties by hand*

Now they are planted using a big machine which opens the drill, plants and covers the totties. The drills are sprayed with weed killer and that is it. The harvester digs two drills at a time and loads them into a trailer which tips them into a frost free shed.

## Tottie Howkin'

I considered this to be the worst job o' the year. Times were bad not only for the farmers, but unemployment was rife in the towns, and men and women were desperate for work. There would be about one hundred who had walked up from Greenock about 6.00 a.m. before we had the morning milking done.

Sometimes we started fifty and turned away fifty. To keep fifty working we yoked three horses in the digger and dug both ways. The workers were happy with two shillings (10p) a day plus two teas and a good dinner. We used a spinner type digger with a screen fixed on to keep the totties from scattering too wide. They were then picked up by hand. My job was to measure out the stretch each had to gather. This could be quite a job when the drills were lengthening or shortening. It was hard to be fair and keep everybody happy. When their baskets were full, the totties were emptied into the carts and taken to a pit prepared in the field. They were couped in and built up to a peak at the top, sloping from about four feet wide at the bottom. They were then covered with wheat straw, and then about six inches of soil. The straw was to keep them dry and the soil to keep out the frost. Later on when the digging was finished we went back and added another six inches of soil, and some severe winters it was all needed. Sometimes when the price fell because of surplus, it would have been better to have sold them straight off the digger. One very bad year some farmers opened up their pits to let in the frost, because they would have lost money dressing them. Supply and demand ruled the market, and I think it always will.

The totties were about the only crop we got paid for directly. The brock (small or scabbie) were fed to the cattle or pigs. All other crops were devoured by the cattle and most of the proceeds came back by the milk cheque. The lifting (or dressing) from the pits could be a cold job. At that time we used a wee round riddle and a scree. The brock went through the riddle down the scree. The totties left on the top of the riddle were put into baskets then into bags and weighed. They were then loaded into carts with big wooden wheels, then loaded on the lorries or taken to a frost free shed.

## Kale

Marrow stem kale was another crop we grew for the dairy kye. It was a good milk producer and grew a heavy crop per acre, but it was unpopular with the workers. It was cut as near the ground as possible and the stems were as thick as your arm. The leaves held water nearly all day, so many a soaking we got. It was tied in bunches big enough for two kye. We aimed at the kale being finished before the heavy frost as it could not be stored. When it was finished we fed the kye with turnips.

## The Turnip Crop

The ground had to be worked much finer than the totties. The seed was sown with a machine designed for the job and drawn by one horse. We believed they had to be sown a certain thickness. If the weather was warm and damp they could be ready for thinning in about ten days. We aye talked about thinning the turnips, but singling is right, because it was essential that only one plant was left about ten to twelve inches apart.

Every wee weed had to be cleared away. This was done by hand, with us crawling on our knees. This is how it was done in this district anyway. In some areas where the land was firmer it was done by using a hoe. These drills had to be kept clear of weeds, and were grubbed and scuffed by a machine drawn by a horse.

When well weeded that wee seed grew into a turnip about twelve to twenty pounds in weight. I suppose I should be calling them swedes, but we aye caud them turnips. They are supposed to be 90% water, but valuable water it is and dairy kye need plenty of water, for it takes water to make milk.

They were left in the ground until October. We pulled the turnip out of the ground and with a big knife we whacked off the shaws and the soil. We dropped them in rows, one turnip at a

*Jimmy drilling*
*for turnips*

time, and there were thousands of them. This either made your back strong or nearly crippled you. Four drills of turnips were made into one row. The rows were spaced so that a horse and cart could go between them.

When loading the turnips a hardy man was expected to land two turnips in the cart, have two in mid air, and then the next two in his hands. He had to be fit to keep that up till the cart was full. The horse moved on and stopped by being spoken to. Great, clever animals they are. We were so used to shouting "woe" to the horse, -that when we became modern and got a tractor, no matter how loud we shouted, the stupid thing never heeded. They were carted off to the steading and piled into great heaps about 20 feet high. We barrowed them into the byre in the winter, where the kye were tied two to a biss. They had individual troughs. We carried in a big basketfull between two.
I can tell you, it did yer hert guid to hear twenty or thirty kye munchin in tae their neeps (turnips).

### Advanced way with Turnips
We had always thought that turnip seed had to be sown at a certain thickness. Now precision seed is sown by a seeder which sows single seeds at whatever space you like. The drills are sprayed with weedkiller. This modern machin-

ery means no singling, no hoeing and no grubbing. Now a machine draws along, lifts the turnips, tops and tails them and loads them on to a trailer. A tipping trailer is used so that they don't even need to be graiped off.

You might think that all this is progress, but what about all the men who have been put out of work? It's getting to the stage that if you had the where-with-all to buy all the modem machinery, you would not need a farm at all.

## Preparing for the same all over again

Out comes the plough again, pulled by two horses. We put a straight line of poles up and this was to guide us as we drew a feerin. We then set the plough for a shallow fur up the field, came back with the same depth, and threw it up close to the first fur. When we completed this, it was called a bout. The plough was set to make the second bout a bit deeper, then the third one deeper still. We carried on at that depth. It was measured from the inside of the thumb to the tip of the fingers.

The idea of the alteration of the depth being so that we were left with a level job and not a big hump. We kept going round this feerin until we had what we caud a gatherin' thirty yards wide. We did the same again away across the field, leaving thirty yards between and this was caud a scaling. The finish of the scaling was caud a hint. In making the hint the plough had to be adjusted again or we would end up with a big ugly hollow in the field.

I have seen six or seven strong men following the plough with picks and pinches, digging out the stones. I've mind of a man from the agricultural department coming in one day and saying he never saw anything more like a bombed city. I have blasted as many as two hundred rocks in a twelve acre field. This is where the material comes from for making the dry stane dykes.

It was a great job ploughing with the horses and they were good company. Making the seed bed was very interesting work, and it was surprising how we got across the field, considering the fact that the fur was only seven inches wide.

When we were very young we used to go out to meet the ploughman coming in from the field. If the horses legs were very mucky, we walked them up the burn. Fresh cold water was bad for causing hacks on their legs, so we rubbed them with whale oil. Another thing we enjoyed was when father arrived at the school with the snow-plough (a home-made one pulled by three horses).

## The Silage Crop

There was a time I thought I would move with the times and try silage. These were early days and silage had not been proved. Indeed a neighbour o' mine said that one midden was enough about any farm. That was his opinion o' a silage heap.

I carted stones and made a big pit (see photo) and worked with silage for a few years, but being a bit auld fashioned I went back to turnips and hay. The stones I used for the pit were all carted out to the fields and I built dykes with them. I must admit that great progress has been made in making good quality silage, but at great

*Building the silage pit*

expense. The machinery is <u>very</u> expensive. In many cases it has taken over from the hay, but we still need good quality hay. It is just bottled sunshine, and is worth all the quiling and rucking.

With all the grain, totties, turnips and hay safely stored. you might think that life would be a bit easier. Nae fear, there was always something needing done. We loaded up the gig with men and scythes, and went to the hills to cut rashes. When I was fourteen, I was trying to keep up with the men. I was knocking my pan in, and all I could get was a BSc (brush, shovel, and cart).

*Pit full, rolling with a tractor*

*James Black*

My brother, Hughie, could sit in the house with a book, even when the sun was shining, but he got his M.A. with honours. Another thing we did on wet days, was to go and dig out rabbits. They were quite a menace. Mother and Auntie had all the rabbits to gut, clean and cook, and some very wet clothes to dry. They had no washing machines or spin dryers in those days. I can still picture them with the old washing boards, rubbing away. In the spring there would be about six women with their skirts rolled up to their knees, tramping blankets in tubs. The feeding for the cows was scalded and steeped in big coolers because the bran etc. would have swollen inside them. This sloppy food would have given them some of their water. It was carried to them twice a day in big pails containing three gallons each.

It takes a lot of water to make milk, and even with all that water in their feed, every cow had to be unchained at midday for a drink at the burn.

*A rare  occurrence: an Ayrshire cow with triplets with my grandson, Iain*

# seven

# Interesting Characters

Life wasn't all work and no play, we had a lot of fun too. Water fights were a regular occurrence, even over the roof tops. It is a wonder we hadn't more accidents. One young man jumped quite a height in desperation. I would like to tell you a bit more about him. He was a game-keeper's son who lived nearby. He came to me looking for work and I said to him, "Well Andy I'm fairly well staffed the noo, but come doon on good days, but I'll no need you when it's wet". Well, it wasn't long till there was a vacancy and Andy was needed full-time. He tells the story that there was never a wet day all the time he was there - at least not too wet to work!

One day I had him helping me with a fence. The posts had been steeped in a tank of creosote which can be a bit nippy. I was using the mell to hammer them in, and I would tell him to keep in close, and make sure he held them straight. Before long Andy looked as if he had spotted fever, as he was splashed all over. You should have heard him the next morning. He said he was in every schuch (ditch) between Auchen-foyle and Harelaw, looking for water to cool him down.

I won't tell you all the tricks we got up to, but they were so numerous that Andy said he would get even with me one day, even if he had to wait till he got me in a wheel-chair. A few years ago I was at Inverclyde hospital to get a plaster on a broken bone. I was being wheeled out to my car, when who appeared but Andy in his uni-form. Aye, you guessed right - he was an ambu-lance driver. I happened to see him in the distance, and shouted, "Naw, naw Andy. I'll walk hame before I'll let you near me". He thought his chance had come to get his own back on me. I think the folk round about were wondering what was going on. That is just a wee sample of the fun we had together. Sadly, Andy has since died. In accordance with his wishes, his ashes were scattered in the fields at East Green.

Then there was old Hughie who was a real auld down-and-out. He had no friends except when he had a few bob in his pocket. He used to stagger home on a Saturday night, giving the impression he was more drunk than he really was. His bed had a wooden frame with boards across it, so when Hughie was away trying to make himself happy, some bad boys were see-ing to it that the boards had very little grip on the edge. You can imagine what happened when Hughie got into bed. Sometimes he spoke a different language, which I couldn't spell, and my pen would refuse to write. One day, Jim Andrew, the vet, came in laughing. He said, "I met old Hughie bringing in the cows, and he was speaking about ten different languages". We had a lot of fun, but it was all in a good cause, because Auchenfoyle was often referred to as the home for incurables. This wasn't really the case, because many cases of real depression were cured there. One of them was D. Henderson and he wrote a fair bit of poetry.

*I didn't believe in boys having long hair*

One verse I remember is:

*Man dear, Auchenfoyle is a wonderful sight,*
*Where men are draining from morning till night.*
*There's Charlie and Paddy and Matthew and Tam,*
*Aye, they're all there, aye, awe tae a man.*

Another verse of the same poem was about what uncle used to say:

*And this is hoo the country's goin' din,*
*The young yins are a' tae blame.*
*They'll no' get up in the morning,*
*And for that they should think shame.*

Another character was Robert Steel (nicknamed Sha). He would never tell a lie unless the truth didn't suit! When I would take him to a gospel meeting, he would make his escape when we got up to sing. He told me about the time the police searched his house, and found stolen goods. He got into trouble, but said to me, *"Don't worry, it'll never happen again"*. Here was me thinking I had got through to him at long last, when to my surprise and horror he said, *"I'll be mair carefuller the next time"*. It wasn't so much the bad grammar that shocked me, but the fact that there was going to be a next time!

## ten
# Observing the Sabbath

T here was no more work done on a Sunday than was absolutely necessary. The animals were fed and the cows milked etc. We were brought up to regard Sunday as a day of rest.

I remember one very wet year, the corn stood in stooks for weeks, battered and soaked. It cleared up on a Saturday, with the wind and sun drying the corn nicely. On the Sunday, many fields in the district were cleared, and I can tell you it was quite a test for us. But God said in His Word, *"Them that honour Me I will honour"*. I set my alarm for twelve o'clock midnight, went into the bothy and pulled the covers off the boys. We went out to the field and caught the horses, yoked the wagons, and got started on the work. We had a lot of corn stacked before daylight. The old shepherd who lived up the hill could hardly believe his eyes in the morning. He called them the fairy stacks. We worked till twelve o'clock that night, which was a round of the clock, and it was well worth it, because the harvest was secured.

# eleven  The Milk Run

Milk prices weren't too good, and we thought we would try to retail it in Greenock. At that time Willie would be nineteen, John nearly eighteen, and I would be sixteen. It was a big step for country yokels like us. We got some bills printed and went to canvas in Greenock. I'll never forget coming doon yon twilrlie stairs, and my heid wis turned. I couldn't remember where the motor was. It was either the twirlie stair or the nice wee lassie that answered the door that knocked me out. I can mind fine that the name on the door was Green, and I thought that Black and Green go well together. I think I must have lacked courage to pursue the matter. Maybe she thought it was me who was green, for she never gave me an order. Not even to get down the stairs.

These were tough times. Murn went to the agricultural college to learn how to make butter from milk instead of cream. We sold butter and sour milk three times a week. We thought this would help to build up the run. We took cans of milk with taps on them, and went round the streets ringing a bell. We had some scattered customers here and there, but had very little success for a long time. John and I went for some months, then Willie went for about a year. That was enough for him, and as soon as I was seventeen, I took over. I had been watching the rest o' them driving, and had pinched wee shots at the wheel, so off I went into the big bad world.

*Part of the hand milking team (from the left):*

*Chrissie Bain, Willie Black, Murn Black, Jennie Black, Tommie Ross, Mary Black*

Things went quietly for about two years, building up a fair wee run. At this time, we went with milk twice a day. I would be in Greenock from the back o' six in the morning, till about eleven o'clock. I went back with warm milk straight from the cow, just after four in the afternoon. A lot of these people are living yet too! (despite the fact that the milk wasn't even cooled, never

*James Black*

*Ready for the road: the night milk run with the milk boys Jimmy Smith and Johnny Glover c.1935*

mind pasteurised!) The milk was measured out with a pint measure into the customer's jug. One day, a braw lassie appeared! Another customer caught me looking at her and said, *"There goes Miss Moodie, she's very goody, goody, but keep your eyes off her because she's already got a boyfriend".* I didn't see much of her on week days but she came out with her milk jug at weekends and holidays. I began to think, then to enquire about her. I found out that her grandfather was a farmer, and I thought to myself, *"Aye, farming will be in her blood".* I found out too that her romance was over, and I said to myself, "Jimmy, get your skates on". I asked her up to Auchenfoyle.

It wasn't long till I gave her a stool and luggy, and had her milking. She did very well, and would have put some farmers' daughters to shame. So you see, it was thanks to the milk run that I met my bonnie wife.

*The apprentice farmers wife*

*James Black*

*Tha man that gets*
*A guid, guid wife,*
*Gets gear enuch,*
*For tho' he spend,*
*He'll hae tae the end,*
*If the wife be ought.*

*But the man that gets*
*An ill, ill wife,*
*Gets care enuch,*
*For though he spare,*
*He'll aye be bare,*
*If the wife be naught.*

The girl in the photograph below has proved the
first verse to be true.

*The courting days*

---

*The Jersey cow: quality milk*

*James Black*

# twelve     The Cousins

W ith father marrying so late in life, our 'cousins' families were about our age, and many of them came about Auchenfoyle a fair bit. Mum was a good organiser of games, and we had a lot of fun. I must mention Betty MacDonald. She was reared at Auchenfoyle as was her mother before her. Father's sister Lizzie was Betty's granny. Betty's mother was Mary Paton who married Alec MacDonald, and sadly she died when Betty and her brother Ronnie were quite young. Betty took over the milk run after me, and is still at it coming on for fifty years later.

Now for the cousins on my mother's side. Her brother James Orr (a clever man) died young, leaving two boys and two girls, all brainy. They visited Auchenfoyle quite a bit on their holidays. They were from Edinburgh, and spoke a different language from us. With their father dying so young, it was a struggle for their mother, but they all had good brains, and won bursaries.

Jackie was governor in a province in India before the independence, then he went into the gold business. Leslie was a head master in Canada. Jean was crippled with arthritis from an early age.

*Jenny Black and Betty*

*James Black*

What a spirit she had, and still has. She reared a family of four, a minister, a doctor and such like. Marie married an Englishman och, he's a' right for a' that. He was Dean of Strathclyde University, but it didna' make him big heided. He is coming on wi' the Scots language. I had him reading my Scots New Testament, which Andy and Anna gave me a few years ago.

Mother's other brother, Robert, married late in life, and left a young son and daughter. Robin, the son, is still in Gateside Farm where my mother was born. His father and mine left matrimony a bit late, but I don't think Robin will pluck up the courage to take such a plunge. His sister, Ruby, married a prosperous, hardworking farmer, and they have brought up three very nice girls. They are the Laird family.

Mother's sister, Janet, had two boys. John was in banking before he took up teaching. Joe was keen on sport, and played football for Rangers before he went to Canada. He qualified as a professor of physical education. He married a Canadian girl and he and Eleanor settled in Vancouver. (It looks as if my brains were shared among my cousins! I just had to work hard for a living).

*Joe and his bride
visiting Auchenfoyle
on honeymoon*

They came to Scotland for their honeymoon, but poor Eleanor had difficulty with our language, especially mine. Joe came back a few times, and he and I had many a great laugh together.

*James Black*

# thirteen **The Green**

F ather had known that it was likely that we
boys would some day need a farm of our
own. He bought The Green, which is about two
and a half miles nearer the village of
Kilmacolm. It had been owned by one family
for three hundred years. The Green consisted of
the usual steadings plus a hundred acres of quite

*The Green*

good land, plus many big stones. With we boys being so young at the time, the house was let, and the land grazed and worked as a unit with Auchenfoyle.

I might have been a bit slow about MY marriage because it took Hitler to shove me on. We were married within a month of war being declared. It was no wonder the tongues waggled - *"a bit of a hurry"*. We did not have a big wedding as May's father died about eight weeks before. On the 27th September 1939 we were married, (and as this is being written, we

Back row from left: *John, Jimmy, Jenny, Hughie, Mary, Willie.* Front row: *Mother, Grannie Orr, Murn*

*Jimmy and his wife on their wedding day*

have just celebrated our 66th anniversary).

Everybody who owned land had to plough up a proportion and grow crops. Oh aye, farmers were much appreciated at such a critical time. Winston Churchill referred to them as, *"Ye hardy sons of toil, upon whose back was placed the burden to feed the nation".*

Some years later, I bought another one hundred and eleven acres from a neighbour - Mr. Cameron. This meant altering the steading at The Green, because having doubled the dairy herd, we had to widen the young beasts' byre to meet sanitary requirements. We made the old stable, loose box and barn into a big long byre which held fifty six cattle. We managed to do all this work ourselves, while keeping everything else going. Some years later, a neighbour sold us another one hundred and forty acres. All this time I had the rent of Gateside Farm too.

Some years later we built a big slatted shed for fat cattle, 240 feet long, thirty feet wide at one end and sixty feet wide at the other, to house 150 cattle. Having bought so much land, the steading was out of proportion.

*A do-it-yourself job: building a new shed*

*James Black*

Facing page and above: *What kind of cow-boy will he be?*

## The Sheep

All these acres of land made it possible for me to increase my sheep numbers.

I had never been without sheep, but had to cut down my numbers considerably when I came to The Green as I only had a hundred acres for grazing the dairy stock and their followers as well as the crops.

Sheep need scope it has been said and I agree that a sheep's worst enemy is its neighbour.

I have always enjoyed working with sheep, and still do. Lambing is a very busy time, but very interesting too. They were all lambed outside, rain, hail or snow:- a day and night job. Nowadays there are many big sheds being built for lambing.

There are many new breeds now, but they would not last long on the Scottish hills. I don't think that the hardy black-faced sheep will ever be replaced.

The clipping was all done by hand shears. The sheep were lifted on to stools made for the job. The fleeces were rolled up and bagged. Great big bags hung from the roof, and they were tramped and tightly packed, then sent to the wool merchant.

*Gathering up and learning young*

*The sheep were all clipped by hand*

*Anna helping with the lambing*

## fourteen
# The War Years

The war years were tough going. Land girls were replacing experienced men, and they did a good job. The bombs were falling quite near us with Greenock and Port Glasgow shipyards being the targets. We could see the reflection of the flames from the fires in Greenock, against the walls at The Green. Many people were hiding in the railway tunnels, because they were being shot at from the air.

We had an old lorry at the time, and it came in very handy to drive many people up to Auchenfoyle and The Green. Many a night there would be over three hundred folk lying in sheds of all kinds, including the piggery, fur coats and all! How thankful they were too. The back was blown out of the hay shed at Auchentiber, by a land mine. That is less than a mile from Auchenfoyle, so it was very fortunate it didn't land there, with all these people sleeping there. At The Green, the steading and the house were packed too. Every room was full, with people lying all over the place.

Later on, nearer the end of the war, we had a few German prisoners of war. Some of them were farmers, and very good workers they were too. I had a letter recently from one of them, who is over ninety now.

*German prisoners of war*

During the war, the schools released children to come up to gather totties. This is how Lily came to be at Auchenfoyle. In spite of being fairly clever at the school, and against her folks' advice, she came to work and live there. She worked hard for a good number of years, and still lives there.

The war created more work, but, before it times were very hard about Greenock and Port-Glasgow. Unemployed men were up pestering as for work at two shillings (10p) per day. Many a time at tottie howkin' time, there would be a hundred men waiting before we finished the milking at six o'clock in the morning. Sometimes We started fifty, and turned fifty away. It was very hard to do that when men were so desperate for work. The ones who were taken on were well fed, and they greatly appreciated it.

The following poem was written by Jack Clark, one of the many Greenock people who took refuge at 'The Green' having been bombed out their houses:

## The Riley

*A ken a lad ca'd Jimmy Black,*
*A brawer lad there ne'er was seen,*
*As ploughin'' grund he had the nack,*
*His mither gaed him auld 'East Green'.*

*Tae 'Auchenfoyle' a mile or twa,*
*Each day he had tae tak the milk,*
*He carried back a bale o'straw,*
*A yow, a sow, or sic like ilk.*

*Yae day a hawker passin' bye,*
*A braw like motor had for sale,*
*And seein' Jimmy thought he'd try,*
*So forthwith went to tell the tale.*

The outcome was the car, a Riley,
Was destined as poor Jimmy's own,
As hawkers are this one was wily,
And Jimmy reaped what he had sown.

The wife and Jimmy - runs this story,
Set forth tae Greenock twice a week,
While flauntin' their begotten glory,
Assumed indifference mild and meek.

Comin' back yae day frae Greenock,
Was sittin Jimmy all alone,
Hurrying for the auld time Bannock,
Or maybe fist a tattie scone.

When all at once at Gryffe Road End,
A lorry loomed frae out the mist,
The driver failed tae tak' the bend,
And hit the Riley full amidst.
Oot Jimmy jumped a wee bit rattled,
Whit, the why, the where, the when,
For proper words his brain it battled,
Why ever born were sic' like men.

The Riley stood all quite forlorn,
The front wheel springs were bashed to bits,
The door frae aff the side was torn,
Enough to try puir Jimmy's wits.

But strange enough the car was able
Tae tak' him still upon his way,
And Auchenfoyles stately gable,
Was loomin' half a mile away.

*Bale wire fetched frae oot the shed.*
*By willin' hauns at Auchenfoyle,*
*While Jimmy he was put to bed,*
*And gi'en a dose o' castor oil.*

*Appearance o' the car was harmed,*
*But Jimmy for it had a use,*
*His heart still tae the Riley warmed,*
*Tho' it had got a bit abuse.*

*It carried then the mornin's milk,*
*And fetched back the puckle corn*
*A yow, a sow, and sic' like ilk,*
*That Riley noo it wadna scorn.*

*A claukin' hen had ta'en a likin',*
*Tae this car o' 'East Green' fame,*
*And when the settin' sun is strikin',*
*It mak's its roost and ca's it hame,*

*Then the Riley got aggressive,*
*Knocked down dykes and telepoles,*
*Thought it had the right possessive,*
*Tae chase puir rabbits doon their holes.*

*But it tried it once too often,*
*Noo it's in a sorry state,*
*A canna tell the truth for laughin'*
*For fegs it's noo a midden gate.*

*And Jimmy while he sups his purridge,*
*Reflects upon wi' one desire,*
*And thinking noo withoot demurrage,*
*He hadn't used that dashed bale wire.*

Above: *This shows the depth of snow on the road as it kept drifting off the fields*
Facing page top: *sledging the milk when the road was blocked for six weeks*
Facing page bottom:*This lorry was being taken for repair as the work was piling up with the road being closed for so long*

*Auchenfoyle brae*

*James Black*

# fifteen
# The Winter of 1945

## sixteen
# Escapades and Leisure

I enjoy a stormy sea, whether it's in a boat or just to swim in. I can't explain it, but when the storm gets up and the sea gets rough, I feel I'm being drawn into it. On such a day I went to The Meigle, down near Largs and the waves were great. Soon one big wave got me side on and out went my top set of teeth. Between burning the roof of my mouth with porridge, and trying to chew ham the next morning, it was no use. I got May to look up the times of the tide in the Greenock Telegraph, so that when the tide went out I could go and have a look. Believe it or not, among all the wee white stones I found my teeth! By way of celebration, I took off my clothes and went back in.

My two brothers and myself in our early teens, when young, strong and daft, yoked three horses in a slype and sledged big boulders into the Gryffe down the burn a bit from a waterfall. It was an ideal place for a swimming pool. We dammed it up till we had fully six feet in depth. It was well used and it is a wonder we had no serious accidents.

*After my swim in
the North Sea*

Andy - no doubt you'll have noticed him being referred to in the book - had to rescue Susie the maid one night. He declares he found her sitting at the bottom of the pond blowing bubbles. She was not amused. Somebody had shoved her under.

We're sometimes plagued with foxes and from time to time we'd have a shoot. One day I had to take a friend to the hospital and was too late for the start of the shoot. I had no gun with me but decided to join them anyway. Gordon MacKay and myself went into the wood to chase the foxes out while the rest of the men with guns surrounded it. We came across a fox lying very life like, and Gordon having his gun levelled it, and prepared to shoot. Just then I noticed that it was dead. I shouted, *"Haud on Gordon, it's deid"*. So between us we did a wee mock hunt. Gordon was shouting, *"Run Jimmy, catch it, catch it."* This was all for the benefit of the men surrounding the wood, so when I appeared out of the wood with the fox over my shoulder, they were dumfoonered.

I was in Largs at a funeral about two years later, and as we went back to our cars, the undertaker came over and spoke to me. I was curious to know how he knew me. He said to me, *"Do you remember the shoot when you came out o the wood with a fox and you had no gun? Many a night I lay in bed wondering how you did it"*. I felt duty-bound to satisfy his curiosity.

Well that fox served me well. A frightened young lady ran from her hen house screaming for help when she found it there. A brave man ran to her rescue with a shovel, smashed it over the head, and promptly declared it to be dead. This happened a fortnight after it had been found in the wood. The next place it turned up was in a hen house in Wemyss Bay and got me into trouble. The young wife said the hens got such a fright that it completely put them off the lay. I didn't mean that to happen, and I gave her some eggs as a peace offering. I also did a bit of trick photography with it.

There is a young man who at one time was a bit depressed and came to me for a job. He must have been real bad to want that. We've had some fun over the years. Every time he comes to visit Andy, my son-in-law, he locks his car, because fairly often something happens to it. One day he called at dinner time and somebody tied a wee dead lamb to the mirror on the passenger side of his car. He got into his car and drove merrily through all the villages to Paisley where his office is, and parked his car opposite an old folks' home.

Someone from there observed this unusual sight and phoned the police, so before long our friend was called out to the car and questioned about his recent movements. After he had told them all the firms he had visited, they asked him where he had got the dirt on his car. He told them he had visited a farm in Kilmacolm. They asked him to go round the other side of the car, and on seeing the dead lamb, our friend exclaimed, *"Jimmy Black did that"*.

Now just try to imagine oor wee freen' who was nearly as broad as he was tall, standing quaking between these two big polis-men, waiting on the hand-cuffs appearing. Not until he bent doon tae the wee lamb (not that he had far tae bend) did the polis say (aye, the big stern one): *"What are you listening to?"* Says he: *"It is singing a wee song. It goes like this: "There will never be another you (ewe)".*

This completely changed the whole atmosphere. They then asked if they could go into his office and phone this man. He said yes, but assured them that they were wasting their time. May shouted to me that the Paisley police wanted to speak to me on the phone. The officer came away with a lot of rubbish about sheep stealing. Then he said, *"We are keeping this man in a holding cell".* I could hardly speak for laughing, but I managed to say, *"What do you want me to do about it, come up and bail him oot or something? Och, just keep him there. It'll dae him good."*

The policeman asked him what age this man was and he told him I was seventy. *"Will you get your own back on him?"*
*"No fear, there are only two men who can lift me off the ground with one hand and he is one of them."*

Another time, I landed this poor chap in the middle of a field with what he thought was a big wild bull. He doesn't really trust me now. He and his wife still speak to me but they got quite a fright one time when they thought I had put a stick of gelignite under the seat of their car, with just a wee bit showing. I used a wrapper from the real thing, rolled a bit of clay and stuck an old fuse into it, so I suppose it did look real, although they should have known I'm not that bad. They were in Kilmarnock shopping when they discovered it, and they panicked, drove to the open country and threw it out. You'll have noticed that I haven't mentioned this chap's name, because Jim Cranson might not be too pleased. Isn't it funny that he has never asked me for a job since?

# seventeen

# Irate Motorists

O ne day I was bringing in some rowdy beasts from the hill. Not being used to a dog, one got very excited and lost the head. It charged across the field, smashed through the dyke with two wires on top and went right into the wing of a nice car.

Well, the two men jumped out, and they were fizzing. The driver was shouting furiously. I gathered that some of his words meant that he was trying to tell me how to work a dog, and the other words weren't in my vocabulary. After a while, I said to him, - *"Is that you finished noo?"* I turned to the other man and said, *"Do you speak English?"* - Says he, *"Aye."* *"Well"*, I said, *"I'll explain to you. Your pal there was just like that beast o'mine. He lost the heid, and wisna'responsible."* - I gave them the name of my insurance company, and wished them well.

Another day I was letting out the kye, (cows) which were chained individually in the byre. (It took a bit o' time.) By the time I got to the last one, the first ones were well up the road. When

I got up to the main road, there was a gentleman parading round his car looking for dents or damage of any kind. He sure went his mile. One of the daft things he said was he knew about cows because his uncle was in that line of business.

He thought that there should be a road up through the field for them. When he could find no damage he started to apologise. He had thought a cow had bumped into it. I said, *"You don't need to apologise, because you wouldn't upset me. If you had danced on your head on the roof of your car, I wouldn't have turned a hair"*. He said, *"Oh, I wish I had your temperament. I've had one of these days"*.

Sometime later, I was at a dentist in Greenock, and when I was giving my name at the desk, a man in a white coat overheard me. Aye, you have guessed right again. He was the man I met on the road. Aye, a real man in my estimation. He started there and then to tell all within his hearing, how he had made a fool of himself that day we met on the road. If I had been in the habit of wearing a hat, I would have taken it off to him. He came in handy from then on, for picking up my teeth if they needed a repair job done. He saved me a few trips to Greenock.

## eighteen
# A Trip to Canada

A ndy my son-in-law, is an evangelist, and
when by was in Vancouver, he visited Joe
Johnson, (the cousin I referred to earlier). Andy
phoned home with the news that Joe was quite
ill, and he suggested to Anna that she should
persuade me to go out to see Joe.

Anna phoned the travel agent the next day, and
found that there were two cheap seats available,
but I had to make my mind up in half an hour.
The result was that I was booked to travel one
week later, but I didn't have a passport, as I had
never been out of the country before. May and
Anna went to Glasgow and managed to get it all
arranged. I was glad of the company of a Perth
farmer on the plane, and I never got out of my
seat till I reached Calgary. From there we flew
over the Rockies to Vancouver. I was glad that
I went when I did because Joe was just like his
old self, but went down fairly fast after that.

I sailed to Victoria, and enjoyed a swim in the
Pacific ocean. I saw some great scenery, and
memorable sunsets. My trip was arranged so

quickly that not many people knew that I was away. I had been doing a bit of work at Auchentiber the day before I went, and Mrs. Howie asked me if I wasn't taking my stab mell with me. *"No"* says I, *"I'll no need it where I'm going"*.

I intended to surprise them, and on the plane wrote a card telling them all the details of the plane, the description of the Rockies etc. I posted it on arrival, and hoped it would be there before I was due home a week later. It was, but do you think they would believe me when I spoke to them about who I met after where I had been? I had to take May up with me before I could convince them. They thought nobody with any sense would go to Canada for a week, and they were sure it was a trick. As if I would do a thing like that!

*Helping this lady who I met after my swim in the Pacific Ocean. She said nobody ever swims here (Victoria BC)*

# nineteen          Blasting

I have already mentioned about the ground being very stony. The new land I bought was no less so. We blasted two hundred stones and rocks in twelve acres. This gave me good experience at blasting, and soon I became a powder monkey. (another name for a shot firer). For me it was relaxation, although some folk think it's a funny way to relax. It is a challenge, and on many occasions has brought great satisfaction.

Sometimes when workmen hit rock, it can stop work going on, and they have to send for the powder monkey. Farmers building new sheds, silage pits and septic tanks sometimes need rock to be blasted. Balfour Kilpatrick, when erecting new electricity poles, often hit rock, and need to call for help. One time a titled lady was to be buried on the top of a hill, and the grave had to be blasted. The hill was so steep that they had to take the coffin up on a tractor and trailer.

Only once was I charged with reckless blasting, and landed in court. However, I got off, and rightly so. It was a big job near Balrossie School, and it was bang, bang every day. The people round about got so fed up with the noise, and maybe the odd fright, and their dogs hiding under the table, that they reported me to the police. They contacted the C.I.D., but I'll spare you the details of the case. I quite enjoyed it, although May didn't. I couldn't afford to quarrel with the police, because I depend on the Chief of Strathclyde police to sign my permit to purchase gelignite on the 15th May, every year. Another job I was on was for a farmer who was building a new shed, and I was a bit short of

Below:
*Before, and*
(opposite page) *After*

*James Black*

covering. I use things like heavy metal plates, fifty-six pound weights and things like that. I asked the farmer if I could use an H iron beam to add a bit of weight. *"Na Na,"* says he, *"I need that tae build the shed. That's one o' the uprights"*. *"Och, it'll dae nae herm"* says I, so we laid it on top of the other covers. What a bang! You should have seen the bend on the beam, and you should have seen his face. I said, *"Never mind, we'll straighten it nae bother"*. I sat it on top of the next shot, and, much to my surprise, and his delight, it looked as good as new. The reason I was so short of cover was that

*This is Neil Caskie whose two wee boys called me Jimmy Bang-Bang*

when blasting near Largs, the fifty-six pound weights went so high, that when they came down with terrific force, they sank out of sight.

My blasting jobs took me over much of Strathclyde region. I had no training. I just picked it up by watching others. I had my own way of carrying out the operation, so much so that when I was approached by the safety man who wanted to come with me to see how it was done, I had not the nerve to tell him in the modern language *"no way"*, but I did manage to put him off. Too well I knew he would not have approved of the roon moothed shovel

*James Black*

replacing the steel helmet and many more things which could be added.

A few times the police were involved. One such occasion was when doing a job for a farmer at Newton Mearns. What I didn't know was that he and his neighbour were not the best of friends, and that is putting it very mildly. When I arrived home after completing the job to satisfaction, the police were on the phone asking if I had been blasting over there and saying I had broken windows on the farm about four hundred yards up the hill. I asked him if he had seen where I had been blasting. He said *"yes"* (it was right beside the public road), so I asked him how come there was no damage done to a farm a few yards away? *"Och,"* I said, *"tell those two men to keep me out of their troubles"*. I heard no more about it. I guessed right. I heard later they were bitter enemies.

Another day I was blasting about four hundred yards from a house. When I came home, two policemen arrived, informing me that I had been accused of blowing the pictures off the wall of this house, *"Just come round here with me"*, I said and I showed them where I had blasted a rock about one foot from the door of a new bungalow and never blew any pictures off the wall. I heard no more about it.

Another time I very near got into trouble was blasting for an extension for a house. Again,

I did not know the owner and his neighbour were the best of enemies. Every time the bang went off, so did the neighbour's burglar alarm: another visit from the police, but needless to say I was well away by the time they arrived and I heard no more about it thankfully.

One job I did not enjoy was over at Lochwinnoch doing a job for the electricity board. When I came home, they came looking for me. They had found a stick of gelignite unexploded. One shot had gone off before the other and was so effective that it had blown the other bit out unexploded. Need I say we were all relieved, including the digger drivers. Since that experience I use cortex; every shot explodes at the same time.

Another time I felt very small was when Scottish Power came and took me over to the hills away above Duntochter. When I tried to cut the fuse wire I was puzzled when my knife would not cut it. I had mistakenly lifted a coil of wire the telephone engineer had left: it was identical to my fuse wire. After a phone call home and a bit of sorting out we got the job done. I think that was my worst experience.

One job I did enjoy was in the Gryffe river at Auchenfoyle. It had to be deepened for draining purposes. I was called in to blast the solid rock that the rock breakers could not deal with. I was letting off thirteen shots at a time, all laced up with cortex. The holes were three feet deep under two feet of water. I'll leave the rest to your imagination.

I refused one job in Kilmacolm. The lady wanted about two feet of rock removed in the basement under the living room. She had been informed that if anybody would do it, it would be Jimmy Black. Well J.B. thought better. You see when I started doing big jobs in and near buildings I enquired about insurance but decided against it for various reasons. Not only were there no windows and only one small door to let the concussion out, plus the fact that it was only about thirty yards from the police station.

There was a lady farmer who knew quite a bit about the powder monkey, but was mair than a wee bit apprehensive about his explosive activities. Maybe she knew just a wee bit too much about him. When labour got scarce she thought it would be a good idea to make things a wee bit easier. I would say a wee bit less slavish. The idea was to do away with the old byre system, and build a big shed with cubicles and a milking parlour.

When the powder monkey saw what was going on, he realised that neither the builders nor the planners knew any mair aboot the kye than the kye knew aboot them. They were going to have eighty big heavy kye climbing half a dozen steps to be milked, then down again every day for years, when all that was needed was the powder monkey with a wee poke o' gelignite tae remove the rock and dig a pit, so that the operator would be on the right level with the kyes' vessels. The finished job was ideal. That is what I call satisfaction in a big way.

Between blasting rocks, digging out stones when ploughing, and building dry stane dykes, I must have handled thousands of tons of stones. Nae wonder May says I'm stone mad.

There are many more stories about blasting to tell, some of which have been recorded on tape. For anyone that would like to hear them, the recordings can be obtained from Sealladh Mor, High Greenock Road, Kilmacolm.

## twenty
# Thankful for Good Health

They tell me I had double pneumonia before I was one year old, before the days of antibiotics - just poultices, bran, linseed and such - cures doctors would laugh at these days. I can mind fine my two brothers and myself all in the bath together and mother coming in with a big jug. It must have held half a gallon of cold water and she poured it over us. Then we got a big spoonful of sulphur and treacle each, a good blood purifier.

Father would put a wee bit of lime, the same lime as was spread in the fields, in our water to drink. He said that it would grow good strong bones.

Fortunately we were healthy. In fact if we ever felt anything wrong we were feart to say anything, because the sure cure for all ills was a good dose of castor oil, and we hated it.

A man said to me fairly recently that he thought I was looking well, and he asked me what I ate. For any of you who have been deluded by listening to advice about certain foods, you

might like to take note. I told him I ate just
about everything which according to some folk,
I should not eat. I ate a lot of butter, dozens of
eggs laid by untested hens. I had fried ham and
eggs every morning for years. I still eat a lot o'
totties and white bread. All my life I've drunk
milk straight from the coo. The water I drink
comes from a spring which overflows all year
round. It travels four hundred yards through a
lead pipe. This water has never been treated in
any way. In spite of, or because of all that, I'm
still enjoying good health at the age of ninety
one.

*James Black*

## twenty one
# Time Moves On

*Time marches on'* my sister, Jenny, used to say when she was a bit harassed and overworked. *"Aye, and we stagger after it"*.

Some say progress marches on and I believe that if you don't move on, there's a good chance you'll go out. The same applies to farming, although there are times when it seems to me that progress is in reverse gear. Some modern ideas I don't like one little bit, but it seems to be that if it's easy, it's right. Some think it's a great achievement to invent a machine which can replace one hundred men. What for? Haven't we seen the result? (Demoralisation). Auchenfoyle, where so many were employed, have only two hired men in regular work.

My brother John left three sons and a daughter. The three boys work Auchenfoyle (and Faulds Farm, which John bought before his death). In these modern times, farmers need to spend thousands of pounds on machinery which doesn't last long, or quickly goes out of date.

The old implements I mentioned earlier, were handed down from generation to generation.

I am taking a back seat now, and handing over to the next generation. Allan is in charge of The Green. He has two sons and a daughter. He asks my advice, and if it suits him he takes it. If it's too auld fashioned, he goes his own way.

While I never agreed that, *"If a thing was good enough for my father then it's good enough for me"*, I always thought it was wise to learn from his mistakes.

John is the eldest of the family, and he sows seed of a different kind. He has spent a lot of time in West Africa. He works as an evangelist, sowing the good seed of the Word of God.

You might think that as I've reached ninety-one years old, I'll have left all the hard work behind me. Not so! For a long time now, I've had very vivid dreams about the work I did in my young days. Nearly every night I find myself back at Auchenfoyle working very hard. I'm glad to waken up for a rest. Sometimes there will be a field of hay just ready for rucking, and it's just about to rain. I'm working really hard to make it safe.

Another dream I often have is when I'm fighting with a wild bull, and sometimes Poor May gets wakened with a mighty kick. So, it looks as if, one way or another, I'll be working till the end.

When I consider the hardships of my father's day, and the trials of the present day, I am thankful I was born when I was. My father told us tales of hardship. Early rising was one of them. He told us that he used to tie bags round the horses' feet so that his father would not hear him passing the bedroom window on his way to Lochwinnoch to the dancing. He would come home very late, or should I say very early in the morning. He would try to slip in quietly, just to be told to go and get the kye in for the milking since he had stayed out sae lang.

Then there were the auld shepherds who went to the drawer and cut a slice o' cauld porridge and away they went to the hill. Nae four wheeled bikes for them. I realise I was born at a guid time, aye the best time. I consider that times are getting worse for farming than they were in my father's day. There is all this non-sense about pollution, environment, sanitary regulations, do gooders releasing mink from their cages and saving foxes. Double tattooing of cattle, keeping records from birth to death, forms and paperwork. Naw, no' for me. I have had the best of it, and would not like to be just starting.

*Twa stanes on the tap o' yin,*
*And yin on the tap o' twa,*
*Weel packit an' weel pointed,*
*An ye'll hae a wa' that'll never fa'.*

*Making use of stones in my spare time after reaching seventy*

*James Black*

*Dressed for a wedding:1994*

The following poem was written by Andy, my son-in-law, when he was in Australia. The cheek o' him!

*Amang a' dates that fill the year*
*There's yin that's way a bin them a,*
*Marked oot, unique; the calendar*
*Withoot it wid seem michty queer.*
*An' that's the wie it aye has been*
*Since nineteen hunner an' fifteen.*

*It's hard tae think, like any ither,*
*This chiel went squakin' tae his mither*
*Who had tae tell him no tae greet*
*When stubble spiked his wee saft feet,*
*Or burnt them on some torry stanes*
*While gaun tae schil wi' a' the weans.*

*But mony a trick did the rascal play,*
*An' roguish pranks frae day tae day;*
*Time efter time his wit wis felt,*
*No least when cuttin' up the belt*
*A lassie cliped; a hammerin' sure*
*Wad help this laddie tae mature.*

*But naw! Ye shouldna' build yer hopes,*
*Sic loutish trends ye canna bend.*
*Jist feel for how each victim copes*
*He'll be like that richt tae the end.*
*An' four score years is proof enough*
*Ye'll never change this kind o' stuff.*

*It's clear that naethin' can be done,*
*An' a' attempts wad be in vain.*
*Jist hope he'll no become unstuck*
*An' end up face doon in the muck*
*For it could happen, aye yer right*
*Too short a fuse on gelignite!*

*It micht o' happened doon yon pit,*
*When he went back once fuse was lit*
*Tae grab his box at double speed,*
*Then rin wi' shovel oor his heid.*
*It's better no tae tell the rest*
*O' muckle tales o' the blasted pest.*

*His birthdays micht o' ended there*
*Or liftin' stanes -for maist oor weichty*
*He'd mak oor heids shake in despair*
*For fear he'd never reach bein' eichty.*
*But noo he has, an' whit a wunner,*
*He's proved us wrang, the stubborn s------!*

# The Sealladh Mor Broch

This is a Broch. The Scotch Dictionary describes four or five different styles of Broch. This is my own style, similar to the one I saw in a garden centre. It took about two weeks to build, having to cart the stones from the hill. The mossy ones on the cope come from the glen. They give it an ancient look. I completed it on my ninetieth birthday, so you see, May was right when she said I was stone mad! I hope to spend some nice days in it with her when I decide to take <u>early</u> retirement.

# Index